iWitness
BIBLICAL
ARCHAEOLOGY

Written and Designed by
Doug Powell

Published by
Apologia Educational Ministries, Inc.
1106 Meridian Plaza, Suite 220/340
Anderson, IN. 46016
Manufactured in the USA
First Printing: May, 2014

apologia.

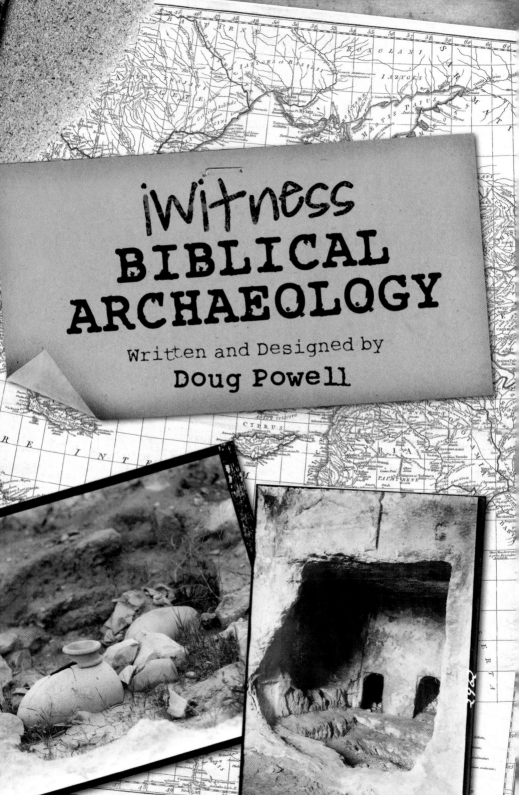

iWitness
BIBLICAL ARCHAEOLOGY

Written and Designed by
Doug Powell

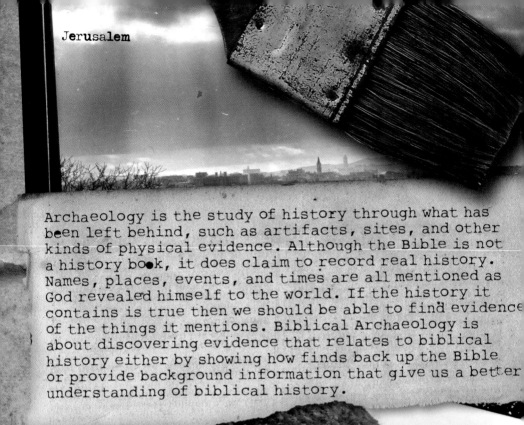

Archaeology is the study of history through what has been left behind, such as artifacts, sites, and other kinds of physical evidence. Although the Bible is not a history book, it does claim to record real history. Names, places, events, and times are all mentioned as God revealed himself to the world. If the history it contains is true then we should be able to find evidence of the things it mentions. Biblical Archaeology is about discovering evidence that relates to biblical history either by showing how finds back up the Bible or provide background information that give us a better understanding of biblical history.

Excavation at Lachish

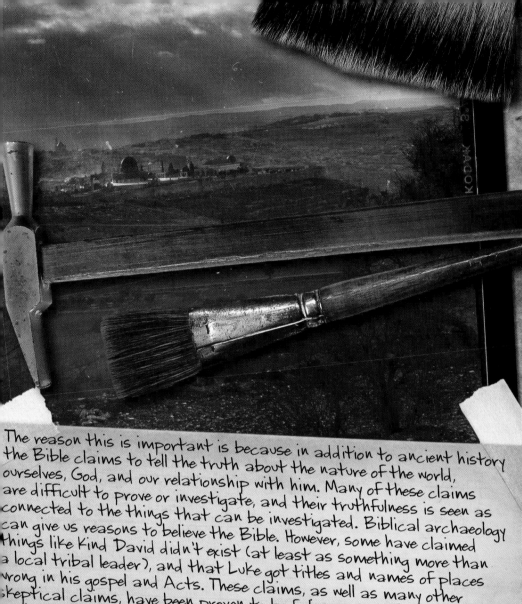

The reason this is important is because in addition to ancient history the Bible claims to tell the truth about the nature of the world, ourselves, God, and our relationship with him. Many of these claims are difficult to prove or investigate, and their truthfulness is seen as connected to the things that can be investigated. Biblical archaeology can give us reasons to believe the Bible. However, some have claimed things like King David didn't exist (at least as something more than a local tribal leader), and that Luke got titles and names of places wrong in his gospel and Acts. These claims, as well as many other skeptical claims, have been proven to be false as more finds have been made. But because archaeology is not an exact science and because the evidence is always by nature, fragmentary, the claims about what it confirms should not be overstated. In fact, logically, it is possible for the history of the Bible to be true but the rest of its claims to be false. So, just because the finds show the accuracy of the Bible's history, they don't PROVE the Bible is true. But they do give reasons for trusting the claims of scripture. So grab a Bible, a map, and a shovel, and get ready to travel back in time.

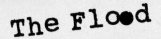

The Flood

Gilgamesh Epic

Date: 7th century BC
Location: Nineveh
 (Kuyunjik, Iraq)
Discovered: 1853
Museum: British
 Museum

Hormuzd Rassam

The way scholars relate the flood stories to the Genesis flood reveals their presuppositions. Some scholars see the Genesis story as based on the myths of the surrounding cultures. They believe the Bible is a man-made book and therefore see Israel as reworking the story to make it fit within their culture and beliefs. However, other scholars recognize these stories may all be related to a historical event that has become mythologized in pagan cultures. They understand that the similarities don't mean the Bible was dependent on the other stories. In fact, the Bible's simpler, straightforward account may be what the other versions were dependent on.

Many ancient cultures have a myth that tells of a great flood killing everyone except the family of a man who was warned by god (or gods) to build a boat. Although there are many differences in the stories from culture to culture, there are some obvious similarities. The Sumerian and Babylonian flood stories are especially important because they record a flood in the same region as the flood in Genesis. The oldest tablets pre-date the writing of Genesis.

Gilgamesh

The Babyloninan flood story of Gilgamesh has several versions that show how it developed over time. The oldest copy to survive is from about 2000-1600 BC. The most complete version is from the 7th century BC. It's contained on 12 tablets found in the palace library of Ashurbanipal in Nineveh. Tablet 11 tells the story of Utnapishtim, who was given eternal life for being obedient to the gods during a catastrophic flood sent to destroy the human race because they irritated one of the gods by being too noisy.

Similarities with Genesis
• God/gods punish humans catastrophic flood
• One man (Utnapishtim/Noah) is warned and told to build a boat for his family and pairs of animals
• Boat lands on mountain
• Birds released to test land
• Sacrifice offered to God/gods

Differences with Genesis
• Noah was not made a god
• Flood lasted 7 days
• Different landing place
• Different design of boat (200' tall cube)

Atrahasis Epic

Date: 17th century BC
Location: Sippar
(Abu Hippar, Iraq)
Discovered: 1880-1881
Museum: British Museum

The Epic of Atrahasis tells a story of how the Mesopotamian gods created human beings because the lesser gods complained about the physical work they had to do in caring for the world. The human race was then created to help them. Like the Gilgamesh epic, one of the gods is annoyed by the noise made by humans, and a flood is sent to destroy them. However, one of the gods warns Atrahasis beforehand. Atrahasis then builds a boat, saves his family and some animals, and makes a sacrifice to the gods after the boat safely makes it through a storm that lasts seven days and destroys the rest of the human race.

This is the best preserved of the Mesopotamian versions of the flood stories.

Another interesting find related to the flood is the list of Sumerian kings. Actually, 15 lists have been found and though there are significant variations between them, they contain much of the same information. The Weld-Blundell Prism is an 8" tall, four sided inscription that gives the longest list. Most of the lists are divided into kings who ruled before "the flood swept over," and kings who ruled after the flood. However, some of the lists don't mention kings from before the flood. The lists also include the length of reigns for each king. The reigns before the flood last far longer than the

SUMERIAN KING LIST

reigns after the flood Not only that, but the lengths are incredibly long. The Weld-Blundell Prism lists eight kings before the flood. The longest reign listed is 43,200 years, and the shortest is 18,600 years. After the flood, the longest reign is 1200 but most are far shorter, with the shortest being 2 years. Among those mentioned after the flood is Gilgamesh.

The Sumerian King list therefore agrees with Genesis on the event of a catastrophic flood, and on the far greater longevity of those who lived before it than those who live after it.

Weld-Blundell Prism
Date: 18th century BC
Location: Larsa (Iraq)
Discovered: 1922
Museum: Ashmolean
Museum, Oxford, England

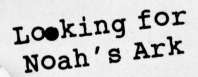

Looking for Noah's Ark

In modern times the search for Noah's ark has focused on Mt. Ararat in northern Turkey. A number of people report seeing it, touching it, and even going in it. Russian engineers are said to have explored it in 1916. It has also allegedly been photographed by pilots stationed in the region. Unfortunately, the stories of finding the ark are often contradictory and describe different locations on Ararat. Even more unfortunately, almost all the photos people have claimed to have taken have been lost. But the biggest problem is that the mountain wasn't called Mt. Ararat until about the 13th century AD (with one possible reference around 500 AD). Ancient tradition doesn't seem to support this mountain as the place where Noah landed. In fact, the Bible does not say the ark landed on Mt. Ararat. Genesis 8:4 says the "mountains of Ararat."

Agri Dagh / Massis / Mt. Ararat

A 1949 photo taken by a spy plane shows a strange object on Mt. Ararat that some have claimed is Noah's Ark.

Mt. Ararat (or Massis) is a single mountain rising above the plains, though there is a much smaller mountain in the vicinity. Another indication Mt. Ararat may not be the place of the ark is that the mountain shows no evidence of a flood.

However, expeditions in search of the ark on this mountain continue. Recently, excavations on the plateau above the Ahora Gorge have indicated a large anomaly about 200 feet long under more than 35 feet of ice. Although the object is not long enough to be Noah's ark, there is another object below the plateau in the gorge. A separate expedition is trying to reach this spot. Whether these two objects are related is not known. And whether or not either object is a ship, let alone, Noah's ark, remains to be seen.

MASSIS

DURUPINAR

In 1948, an earthquake brought what appears to be an enormous ship into view at Durupinar on the Akyayla Range, about 17 miles from Mt. Ararat. This went largely ignored until the mid-80s when it became the focus of some ark enthusiasts. Several theories try to reconcile it with the biblical account. One says the ship could have landed higher up in the valley and slid down to its spot. This theory points to possible ancient stone anchors found not far away. Another theory says there may have been more than one ark built to survive the flood. Few scholars take this site seriously.

The weather conditions allow work on the sites only about one month out of the year. And because it takes a four-day hike to get the equipment to the site, progress is slow. The volitile political situation in the region adds a whole different set of problems.

Another problem is glory hunters who make fake claims of discovering the ark. Many of these frauds were done by taking ancient wood up the mountain and then claiming they found the wood on the ark. However, the wood is always from the wrong region, or not old enough, and the discoverers could never lead anyone back to the ark.

Durupinar
Remains of the ark?
Is this a stone anchor?

Looking for Noah's Ark

continued

200 MILES SOUTHWEST OF MASSIS IS A RANGE CALLED "THE MOUNTAINS OF ARARAT," AND HAS BEEN CALLED THAT SINCE AS EARLY AS 2000 BC. PAGAN, JEWISH, CHRISTIAN, AND ISLAMIC TRADITIONS (INCLUDING THE QURAN) PRIOR TO AD 1300 ALL POINT TO THIS MOUNTAIN RANGE AS THE PLACE WHERE THE ARK LANDED. SOME OF THESE TRADITIONS PREDATE THE BIRTH OF CHRIST. MANY OF THESE TRADITIONS ALSO POINT TO A SPECIFIC MOUNTAIN CALLED "CUDI DAGH," OR MT. JUDI.

PEOPLE WHO CLAIM THE ARK WAS AT THIS LOCATION AND WAS VISIBLE IN THEIR DAY INCLUDE: BEROSSUS (A PAGAN PRIEST IN THE 3RD CENTURY BC), JOSEPHUS (A HISTORIAN IN THE 1ST CENTURY AD), EUSEBIUS (HISTORIAN IN THE 4TH CENTURY AD), EPIPHANIUS (BISHOP OF SALAMIS IN THE 4TH CENTURY), CHRYSOSTOM (ARCHBISHOP OF CONSTANTINOPLE LATE 4TH-EARLY 5TH CENTURIES), THEOPHILUS (BISHOP OF ANTIOCH IN THE 6TH CENTURY), ISIDOR (ARCHBISHOP OF SEVILLE, 6TH-7TH CENTURIES), AL-MASUDI (MUSLIM SCHOLAR IN THE 10TH CENTURY), AND ZAKARIYA IBN MUHAMMAD AL QAZVINI (GEOGRAPHER IN 13TH CENTURY). PIECES OF WOOD HAVE BEEN FOUND AT THE SITE AS LATE AS THE 1800s. SOME OF THE WOOD WAS APPARENTLY TAKEN TO BUILD A MOSQUE IN THE TOWN OF CIZRE.

CUDI DAG

NESTORIAN MONKS BUILT A MONASTERY ON THE SITE THAT BURNED DOWN IN 766. A SHRINE WAS BUILT ON TOP OF IT AND CAN BE SEEN IN THE 1909 PHOTO BELOW. IT IS CALLED THE PLACE OF DESCENT. IN RECENT TIMES IT HAS BEEN TOO DANGEROUS TO TRAVEL TO, MAKING CURRENT PHOTOS UNAVAILABLE.

IN 1953, GERMAN GEOLOGIST FRIEDRICH BENDER WAS TAKEN TO THE SITE AND FOUND A LOAM-LIKE SUBSTANCE HE TOOK SAMPLES OF. TWO TESTS CONFIRMED IT WAS WOOD COVERED BY ASPHALT AND WAS 6500 YEARS OLD.

MASSIS

DURUPINAR

URARTU
(MODERN DAY TURKEY)

Remains of a shrine where a monastary called The Cloister of the Ark once stood. It is now called Sefinet Nebi Nuh (Ship of Noah), The Place of Descent on Cudi Dagh.

The Mountains of Ararat including Cudi Dagh

Egyptian Chronology

The chronology of Egyptian pharaohs is very important because the dating of several other cultures rely on it or refer to it in some way. Archaeological evidence provides some clues, while ancient historians (Egyptian, Greek, African, Jewish, and Christian) provide others. One of the most important sources is the Egyptian historian and priest Manetho who lived in the 3rd century BC. Manetho records the pharaohs as broken into 30 different dynasties, with each dynasty being a family line in most cases. Although there are some periods in which we cannot be certain of the order of the kings, the length of the reigns still gives us a way to make a timeline. The dating is also made in relation to the astronomical phenomenon of the sothic cycle.

The standard understanding of the biblical timeline, however, does not agree with the standard Egyptian chronology. A number of solutions for understading the biblical timeline differently have been proposed that do agree with the standard chronology of Egypt.

The evidence for the standard chronology has begun to face criticism by some scholars. The problems they see include evidence that some pharaohs ruled at the same time in different parts of Egypt, the length of some reigns include co-regency (a period of shared power, such as in the case of a minor ruling with his father), and the imprecision of dating according to the sothic cycle. As a result, the standard chronology may be off by several hundred years. Taking this into account, a revised chronology may give us a more accurate picture of history.

Since the standard chronology was introduced, Old Testament scholars have struggled with the fact that the biblical timeline doesn't seem to sync up with it. The date of the Exodus is one of most important events affected by this. The Old Testament puts the Exodus at about 1440 BC, but the standard chronology makes it around 1260 BC. The revised chronology, however, harmonizes perfectly with the Old Testament, as well as timelines of other cultures, and archaeological evidence such as the dating of the fall of Jericho. Many critics of the Bible's historical claims have pointed to the Exodus as having no proof, but it may be they were looking for evidence in th wrong century.

Using the standard chronology, the pharaoh of the Exodus is most often identified as Rameses II. Other possibilities are Thutmose III and Amenhotep II. This is hard to sync up with the historical claims of the Bible. Exodus 15:19 and Psalm 136:15 state that pharaoh drowned in the Red Sea. And yet the mummies of all these pharaohs are on display in the Egyptian Museum in Cairo, not at the bottom of the sea. Either the Bible is wrong, our interpretation of it is wrong, or there is a problem with the standard Egyptian chronology.

Amenemhet III. Is this the pharaoh whose daughter adopted Moses?

Revised chronology

Using the revised chronology reveals a harmonization of all the evidence. The pharaoh of Moses' upbringing would have been the last king of the 12th dynasty, one without a natural heir. Once Moses fled, the dynasty ended with the king's death. The new pharaoh did not know Moses, and the new dynasty would explain why. Possible pharaohs for the Exodus include Sobekhotep IV, Tutimaios, and Neferhotep I (whose mummy has not been found, though this is not unique).

Mummy of Rameses II

The Exodus

Near the pyramid of Sesotris II is a city called Kahun, where the builders who made the pyramid lived. There is evidence that a large number of these workers were from Palestine and may, in fact, be the Israelites. Flinders Petrie, who excavated the site, found a large number of non-essential household items that seem to show the people who lived there left in a hurry, taking only what they needed. Under the floors of the houses, he also found boxes containing the bones of infants. And unlike later pyramids made of stone, the pyramids these workers built were made of mudbricks. All of these finds agree with the biblical account of the Israelites as workers in Egypt, the killing of infants, and the Exodus. Many of the artifacts can be found in the Manchester Museum.

Drawing of Kahun by Petrie

Almost 400 tablets have been found at Amarna, Egypt. Most of the letters have nothing to do with biblical history. But many of them mention a people called the Habiru who are in Canaan. And the way Canaan is described is very similar to how the Old Testament talks about it during the conquest that followed the Exodus. Since the tablets are dated after the early date of the Exodus, this seems to support the traditional date. However, Habiru may refer to a broader group of people than just the ancient Israelites.

Amarna Tablets

Date: 1365–1335 BC
Location: Amarna, Egypt
Discovered: c. 1887
Museum: British Museum

The Ipuwer Papyrus (also called The Admonitions of an Egyptian Sage) talks about a plague that devastated Egypt. In fact, six of the plagues of Exodus are mentioned by Ipuwer. Some scholars see Ipuwer as a poem, not a history that describes the same event as the biblical plagues. However, the similarities can't be denied.

Like the plagues of Exodus, Ipuwer says the river was blood; people couldn't drink the water; trees, herbs, crops, grains, and fish were destroyed; fire consumed the ground; cattle wandered; darkness was in the land; "he that lays his brother in the ground is everywhere;" all of Egypt cried out with grief.

These obvious parallels show that the Ipuwer papyrus may be a non-biblical record of the plagues in Exodus.

Ipuwer Papyrus

Date: 13th century BC
Location: Memphis, Egypt
Discovered: 1828
Museum: Dutch National
  Museum of Antiquities,
  Leiden, Netherlands

Jericho is important for dating the Exodus because it was the first city conquered after entering the promised land. Many scholars have tried to use Jericho to disprove the Bible by showing that its destruction happened before the Exodus. However, a good case has been made for dating its destruction to 1406 BC, which fits the biblical account perfectly. There was both a city wall and a retaining wall at Jericho. Excavations show the city wall collapsed and fell against the retaining wall, which agrees with Joshua 6:20. The city showed evidence of fire damage, and every room had debris from bricks, wood, and household items. The fire damage happened shortly after the walls fell. Pottery found in the debris helps give such a precise date. Jars still full of grain show the seige was short and that it was not plundered, agreeing with Joshua 6:3-5, 17-18.

Excavations at Jericho.

House of David Inscriptions

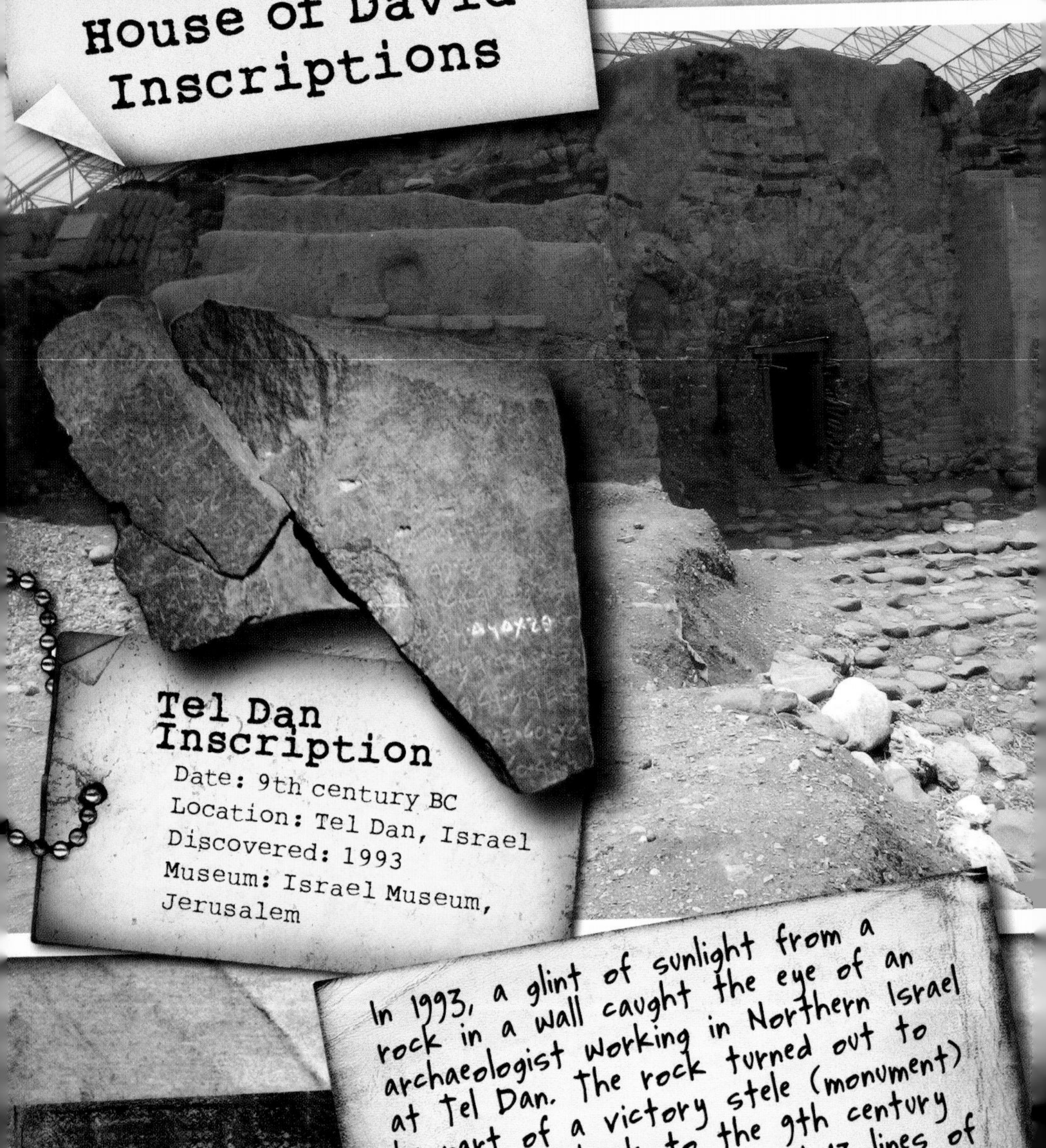

Tel Dan Inscription

Date: 9th century BC
Location: Tel Dan, Israel
Discovered: 1993
Museum: Israel Museum, Jerusalem

In 1993, a glint of sunlight from a rock in a wall caught the eye of an archaeologist working in Northern Israel at Tel Dan. The rock turned out to be part of a victory stele (monument) that dated back to the 9th century BC. The fragment contained 13 lines of text that told of the victory of King Hadad over the city of Dan.

Part of the text includes the claim that the king of Israel was killed as well as someone (the name is illegible) who was of "the house of David." This is the first discovery of a non-biblical text that mentions David.

Over 100 years earlier a medical missionary who had befriended some Bedouins was taken to ruins east of the Dead Sea in Jordan to see what became known as the Mesha Stele or Moabite Stone. The doctor returned to Jerusalem to try to raise the funds to buy it. In the meantime British archaeologist Charles Warren and French archaeologist Charles Clermont-Ganneau found out about the stele. Ganneau sent someone to make a squeeze of the inscription (a technique where wet paper is pressed into an inscription and then allowed to dry, making a cast). Before the squeeze could dry, the Bedouin became suspicious and then violent, causing Ganneau's man to flee with the wet squeeze, which tore into pieces. Then, when the Bedouin found out the Ottoman Empire was helping to recover the stele, the Bedouin decided to destroy it rather than have the Turks assert authority over them. They set a fire under the stele and poured water on the hot stone which then broke into pieces. Over the next decade, Warren and Ganneau found enough pieces to reconstruct 2/3s of the stele. Ganneau then used the squeeze to recreate the missing parts.

The stele contains 34 lines that mark a number of victories by the king of Moab, who fought King Omri in 2 Kings 3. The stone mentions not only Mesha and Omri but also Yahweh. When the definitive translation was finally made in 1994, it was revealed that one of the lines may refer to the "house of David," though part of the name is obscured.

Charles Warren

Clermont-Ganneau

Mesha Stele/Moabite Stone

Date: 9th century BC
Location: Dibbon
   (Near the Dead Sea in Jordan)
Discovered: 1868
Museum: Louvre, Paris

YHWH Inscriptions

Amarah-West

Soleb

The Soleb and Amarah-West inscriptions are not important simply because they are the oldest mentions of Yahweh. Their age is important evidence for trying to date the Exodus.

Soleb Inscription
Date: c. 1400 BC
Location: Soleb, Egypt (Sudan)

Around 1400 BC, Amenhotep III built a temple in southern Egypt at Soleb. It was common for Egyptian temples to have lists of peoples they had conquered. On the base of one of the pillars the list mentions "the shasu of YHWH." "Shasu" is a generic term for a nomadic or semi-nomadic people. Several shasu groups are identified by also listing where they were from. But there is no historical record of a place called YHWH. And even if one is found, it's likely named after the God of the Israelites. And the way the phrase is written, it can also mean "the land of the nomads who worship Yahweh."

This mention in the list of conquered people is the oldest mention of YHWH outside of the Bible.

100 years later, Rameses II built a temple at Amarah-West, not far from Soleb. This temple also includes a list that mentions YHWH.

During an excavation at Thebes, Sir Flinders Petrie discovered a stele over ten feet that that is one of the most important finds in biblical archaeology. It mainly records a victorious military campaign of Pharaoh Merneptah. However, at the bottom of the inscription, the name "Israel" appears. Not only that, but Israel is refered to as an ethnic group, not a place. This is the oldest mention of Israel by name outside of the Bible.

Israel Inscription

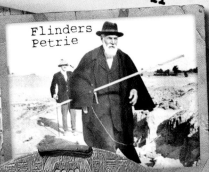

Flinders Petrie

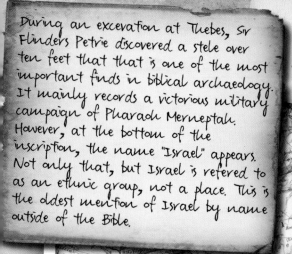

Merneptah Stele

Date: c, 1208 BC
Location: Thebes, Egypt
Discovered: 1896
Museum: Egyptian Museum, Cairo

Sennacherib's Seige of Jerusalem
(finds at Nineveh)

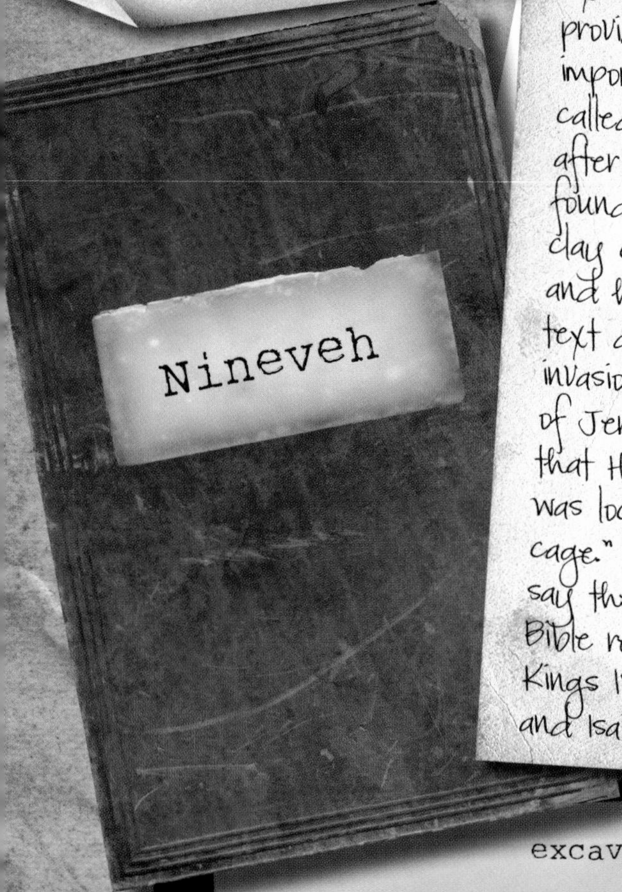

Nineveh

Beginning in the 1830s the excavations at Nineveh have provided a number of very important finds. One of these is called the Taylor Prism, named after the British diplomat who found it. The Taylor Prism is a clay cylinder just over 15" tall and has six sides of writing. The text describes Sennacherib's invasion of Judah and the seige of Jerusalem. The prism says that Hezekiah, King of Judah, was locked up like a "bird in a cage." However, the text does not say the seige was successful. The Bible records the same event in 2 Kings 18:13–19:37, 2 Chronicles 32, and Isaiah 36–37.

excavation of Lachish

Lachish reliefs from the palace of Sennacherib at the British Museum in London.

Since Taylor found this prism, seven more prisms with virtually the same text have been found.

In 1847, the southwest palace of Sennacherib was discovered. It contained a vast display of reliefs on its walls depicting important battles from his military campaigns. One of these scenes was of the seige of Lachish, the battle before seige of Jerusalem. Although the seige is not mentioned in the Bible, Lachish is mentioned in scripture. Sennacherib may have had this seige depicted instead of the seige of Jerusalem because the seige of Jerusalem was not successful.

Taylor Prism

Date: 690 BC
Location: Nineveh
(Nebi Yunus, Iraq)
Discovered: 1830
Museum: British Museum

Sennacherib's Seige of Jerusalem
(finds at Jerusalem)

Jerusalem

Siloam Inscription

Date: Late 8th century BC
Location: Jerusalem
Discovered: 1880
Museum: Archaeological Museum, Istanbul

After becoming king of Judah, Hezekiah decided to break off the relationship with Sennacherib, to whom Judah had been paying tribute for protection. Hezekiah knew this would probably mean Sennacherib would invade Judah, and that's just what he did. But before Sennacherib's army arrived at Jerusalem, Hezekiah prepared the city to withstand a seige. According to 2 Kings 20:20 and 2 Chronicles 32:30, he ordered a tunnel to be dug that connected the Gihon Spring, where Jerusalem gets its water, to what became known as the Pool of Siloam.

Hezekiah's tunnel was discovered in 1838 by Edward Robinson. It runs for 1750 feet, and rather than being cut in a straight line, it winds its way between the two points. In 1880 some boys playing in the tunnel noticed an inscription in the wall. It describes how the tunnel was carved, with two teams of men with pick axes cutting their way toward each other. Apparently, each team had a guide above ground who pounded the top of the rock and the sound would let the team know which direction to go. Ten years later the inscription was stolen. However, it was recovered and placed in the Archaeological Museum of Istanbul.

beginning of the tunnel

Hezekiah's Tunnel

Date: Late 8th century BC
Location: Jerusalem
Discovered: 1830

end of the tunnel

Old Testament History

Artifacts

Nabonidus Cylinder

Date: 6th century BC
Location: Ur (Iraq)
Discovered: c.1854
Museum: British Museum

There have been many finds that don't mention ancient Israel that are still very important for biblical archaeology. Some of these finds talk about kings or nations previously known only through the Bible. Others record history that backs up the events described in scripture.

The Nabonidus Cylinder documents the rebuilding of a temple in Babylon. The inscription mentions Belshazzar, who until this discovery was known only from the book of Daniel.

The Cyrus Cylinder records some of Cyrus's military victories, including over Babylon. It also talks about how he let the captives in Babylon return to their homeland. This backs up the Bible's account of the Jews's return to the promised land found in 2 Chron 36:22-23; Isaiah 45:1-13; Ezra 1:1-3; 6:1-5

The Ishtar Gate was one of the entrances to Babylon. An inscription on the wall mentions "Nebuchadnezzar, King of Babylon." This is how the Bible refers to him in Jeremiah, Daniel, 2 Kings, 1 Chron and Ezra.

Cyrus Cylinder
Date: 539~530 BC
Location: Babylon (Iraq)
Discovered: 1879
Museum: British Museum

Ishtar Gate
Date: 575 BC
Location: Babylon(Iraq)
Discovered: c.1899
Museum: Pergamum Museum,
Berlin

Old Testament History
continued

Lachish Letters
Date: 597 BC
Location: Lachish, Israel
Discovered: 1935
Museum: Israel Museum

Black Obelisk
of Shalmaneser III

Date: 827 BC
Location: Nimrud (Iraq)
Discovered: c.1846
Museum: British Museum

Saul's fortress has been discovered at
excavations in Gibeah.

The Lachish Letters were written just before
Judah was taken captive by Babylon. What they
describe matches what we read in Jeremiah,
Daniel, and 2 Chronicles. They also mention the
name Yahweh.

Other finds refer to kings of Judah or Israel
by name and therefore back up the biblical claims
for their existence and the times they lived.

Hezekiah Bulla
Date: 8th century BC
Location: non-provenanced
(antiquities market)
Published: 2004
Dealer: Archaeological
Center Tel Aviv, collection
of J. Chaim Kaufman

Baruch Bulla
Date: 7th century BC
Location: non-provenanced
(antiquities market)
Published: 1978
Museum: Israel Museum

The Black Obelisk of Shalmaneser III mentions Jehu and even shows him offering a tribute. This is the oldest picture of an Israelite and was made during their lifetime.

The Hezekiah Bulla's inscription reads "Belonging to Hezekiah, (son of) Ahaz, king of Judah."

The Baruch Bulla's inscription says, "(belonging) to Berekhyahu, son of Neriyahu, the scribe." Baruch was the scribe of Jeremiah (e.g. Jer 36:4).

A record of military victories called the Annals of Tiglath-Pileser refers to the kings of Judah. It also records events found in 2 Kings 15 and 16, 1 Chron 5, and 2 Chron 28.

Annals of Tiglath-Pileser
Date: 728 BC
Location: Nimrud(Iraq)
Discovered: c.1845
Museum: British Museum

Dead Sea Scrolls

At the end of 1946 or early 1947, a bedouin shepherd was trying to find a goat that had strayed from the flock near the Dead Sea. There were lots of caves in the area, and rather than going in all of them to find the goat, he threw rocks into the caves to try to scare the goat out. But when he threw rocks in to one of the caves he heard the sound of breaking pottery. After climbing into the cave thinking he might find some kind of treasure, he found several broken jars, some scrolls, and lots of fragments of old scrolls.

The shepherd took the scrolls back to his tent thinking he could use the old parchment for sandal straps. After a year or so, he decided to sell them to a Bethlehem cobbler named Kando who also sold antiquities out of his back room. Kando paid the shepherd 16 pounds (Jordanian) for the first four scrolls. Three more scrolls were also discovered and sold to Kando.

Kando wasn't sure what he had bought, but he knew it was old. He sold three scrolls to another dealer named Salahi. The other four he sold to the Archbishop of St. Mark's monastary.

The cliffs on the northwest side of the Dead Sea where scrolls were found in eleven different caves.

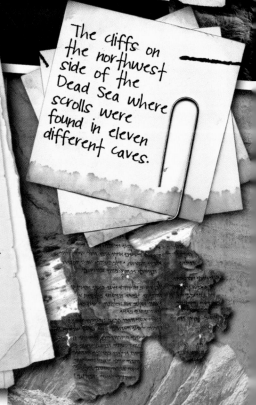

Salahi sold his scrolls to a professor from the Hebrew University named Sukenik. The Archbishop turned down Sukenik's bid for the other four. Instead, he brought them to New York where he actually took out an ad in the Wall Street Journal to sell them. In yet another strange twist, Sukenik's son, Yadin, was in New York the day the ad ran and arranged to buy them for $250,000. Once the news got out that the scrolls were worth so much, both Bedouin and scholars began searching other caves in the area. Eventually, ten more caves with scrolls were found.

Dead Sea Scrolls
continued

The discovery of the Dead Sea Scrolls is easily one of the most important archaeological finds in history. Over 100,000 fragments were found. They contain text from over 900 different writings and books. Some of these books are apocryphal or pseudepigraphal (books wrongly attributed to biblical figures). Other writings mostly had to do with the workings of Qumran, the community that owned, and eventually hid, the writings.

At least 223 of the writings found are copies of books in the Old Testament. In fact,

there is at least one copy of every book in the Hebrew Bible except for Esther. The reason this is so important is because until the Dead Sea Scrolls were found, the oldest copy of the Old Testament was from the 10th century AD. The community of Qumran was destroyed around AD 68, and the oldest fragments are from about 150 BC. So we now have evidence for the text of the Old Testament that is 1,000 years older than we had before. This gives scholars a way to figure out how accurately the text has been copied.

W.F. Albright, one of the first scholars to authenticate the Dead Sea Scrolls.

Ruins of Qumran

Twenty copies of Isaiah were found in the caves. One of them – dated 125 BC – has very little missing from it and is now called the Great Isaiah Scroll. When these copies were compared to the text of Isaiah we used before the Dead Sea Scrolls were found, scholars were amazed at how similar they were.

The text agrees 95 per cent of the time. The few places they are different has to do with spelling variants and simple errors. This shows just how carefully the Jewish community handed down the text. It gives us good reason for trusting the text of the Hebrew Bible as we now have it.

Oldest Old Testament Copies

Aleppo Codex

Date: c. AD 930
Location: Aleppo, Syria synagogue
Museum: Israel Museum, Jerusalem

Although some pieces have been lost or destroyed, the Aleppo codex is the oldest copy of the Hebrew Bible that originally contained all the books. Before being placed in a museum it spent over 500 years in the synagogue at Aleppo, Syria. It's from about AD 930.

The oldest fragments of the Hebrew Bible are part of the Dead Sea scrolls. Some of them date to the 2nd century BC. Every book except Esther was found in the discovery, and no copy was later than AD 68. Probably the most important find is the Great Isaiah scroll, an almost complete copy from about 150 BC.

The oldest quotation of scripture outside the Hebrew Bible was found on a bracelet on the arm of a skeleton in a tomb in the Hinnom valley, outside Jerusalem. The quote is from Numbers 6:24-26 and was written sometime in the 7th century BC.

Hinnom Amulet
Date: 7th century BC
Location: Hinnom, Israel
Discovered: 1979
Museum: Israel Mueum,
    Jerusalem

Dead Sea Scrolls
Date: 2nd cent. BC - 1 cent. AD
Location: Qumran, Israel
Discovered: 1947-1956
Museum: Majority of fragments
    in Israel Museum, Jerusalem

Oldest New Testament Copies

Tischendorf

NEW TESTAMENT NOTES

Codex Siniaticus

Date: 4th century AD
Location: St Catherine's
    Monastary, Sinai
Discovered: 1844
Museum: British Library,
    London

The oldest complete New Testament was discovered by Constantin von Tischendorf in St. Catherine's Monastary at the foot of Mt. Sinai. He claimed to find some old parchments that were about to be burned and recognized them as biblical texts. One of them was what came to be known as Codex Sinaiticus.

The oldest fragment of the New Testament is called P52. It's 3.5" tall and just over 2.75" wide. It contains part of the Gospel of John and is dated about AD 120. This also shows how fast the gospel began to spread around the world.

There are many early writings that quote from the New Testament books. In fact, the early church fathers quoted from the New Testament over 36,000 times in their writings. But the oldest quotation written in stone was recently found carved into the side of Absalom's tomb. It contains Luke 2:25.

P52
Date: c. AD 125
Location: Egypt
Discovered: 1920
Museum: John Rylands
   University, Manchester,
England

Absalom Tomb Inscription
Date: 4th century AD
Location: Jerusalem
Discovered: 2003

Hadrian and Constantine

Inside the Church of the Nativity showing part of the original floor of Contantine's building.

Hadrian knew Christians believed Jesus was born in a particular cave in Bethlehem. So he had the cave filled in, planted a grove of trees on the spot, and dedicated it to Adonis. Constantine had the grove removed and discovered a cave below the trees. He built a chapel near the cave's entrance. Parts of the mosaic floor from his chapel have been discovered under the floor built years later by Crusaders when they expanded the church. There is no way of knowing if this is the place of Jesus' birth. However, the tradition is very strong and early for this location.

Traditional spot of Jesus' birth.

Hadrian had the tomb of Jesus, which was in an old quarry, filled in. Then he built a temple to Venus on top of it. Constantine had the temple knocked down and the area excavated. Below the temple was a tomb that was thought to be the tomb of Jesus. Several tombs were found in the quarry, but one stood out. There may have been graffiti or some kind of marking on it. Constantine built a portico around it. Later, crusaders enclosed the area, including the traditional spot of Golgotha. The tomb has been damaged many times, and is decorated beyond recognition. But there is good reason to believe that the few original parts of the tomb that remain were actually Jesus' tomb.

Traditional site of Jesus' tomb

The Church of the Holy Sepulchre

Constantine's original entrance

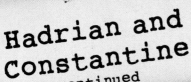

Hadrian and Constantine
continued

**Hadrian
Era Coin**
Date: AD 119

The temple rebuilt by Herod the Great had only been finished a few years when it was destroyed during the Jewish revolt of AD 70. When the Roman army under the command of Titus sacked Jerusalem, they razed the temple and threw the stones off the platform where it was built. Rubble at the base of one of the walls can be seen to this day.

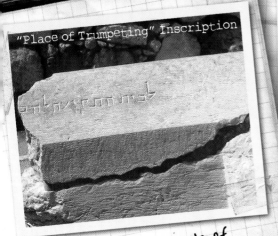

"Place of Trumpeting" Inscription

Rubble from AD 70

There have been a couple of interesting finds in the rubble. One is an inscription marking the "place of trumpeting." The sounding of a trumpet marked the beginning and end of sabbath. Another discovery is of a plaque that warns that no gentiles were allowed beyond a certain area.

**Constantine
Era Coin**
Date: AD 313

During the reign of emperor Hadrian, the Jews revolted again. When it ended in AD 135, Hadrian banned the Jews from Jerusalem and renamed it Aelia Capitolina. He also changed the name of Judea to Palestine. He even tried to erase the holiest sites of both Jews and Christians. In addition to trying to destroy the birth place and tomb of Jesus, he built a temple to Jupiter on the site of the Holy of Holies.

When Constantine came to power his mother, Helena, made a tour of the Holy Land. Although Jews had been kicked out of Jerusalem for a time, Christians had not. And they knew the locations of the places Hadrian tried to ruin.

The exposed rock where the Holy of Holies was probably located. The right side shows the foundation of the western wall. The foundation of the southern wall is also faintly visible. The rectangular spot in the bottom middle is where the Ark of the Covenant may have been placed.

Helena learned that by trying to erase the locations of the temple, the birthplace, and tomb of Jesus, Hadrian had actually marked them. Constantine did not care much about the temple mount, but he had the birthplace and tomb of Jesus restored.

In 638 Jerusalem fell to Muslims who built a mosque where the Holy of Holies once stood. Crusaders took back Jerusalem in 1099 and converted it to a church. But in 1187 it fell again to the Muslims and has remained a mosque ever since. Although the spot of the Holy of Holies has been damaged, there remains some evidence of the original walls, and even the possible location of the ark.

Temple Warning

Date: 1st century AD
Location: Jerusalem
Discovered: 1871
Museum: Archaeological
    Museum, Istanbul

Jesus' Judges

In 1990, bulldozers working on a park near Jerusalem accidentally unearthed a cave that contained 12 ossuaries. These bone boxes were used by Jews for burial between the 1st century BC and the 1st century AD. The cave was apparently the family tomb of Caiaphas, the high priest from AD 18 to 36 who presided over the trial of Jesus. Two of the ossuaries had inscriptions that included the name of Caiaphas. One of them was highly decorated, which may signify the importance or wealth of the person buried inside.

PALESTINE

ILLUSTRATING THE
OLD AND NEW TESTAMENTS.

ACCORDING TO PALESTINE EXPLORATION SURVEY.

BY J. BARTHOLOMEW, F.R.G.S.

Caiaphas Ossuary

Date: 1st centuary AD
Location: Jerusalem
Discovered: 1990
Museum: Israel Museum,
Jerusalem

Pilate Stone
Date: AD 26-36
Location: Casesarea, Israel
Discovered: 1961
Museum: Israel Museum,
Jerusalem

Extra-biblical evidence for the existence of Pontius Pilate turned up in 1961 in Caesarea Maritima. The theater was being excavated when they found a stone in a stairway that had his name and title (Prefect of Judea) inscribed on it. The plaque had marked a temple to Tiberius and had been repurposed when the theater was renovated around the 4th century.

Herod the Great
and
Herod Antipas

When Jesus was no more than two years old, Herod the Great felt threatened enough by him to try to have him killed. Herod, who ruled from 37-4 BC, not only restored the temple in Jerusalem, he completed many other building projects. One of them was the

Herod the Great's tomb

Herodium, a palace/fortress on a man-made mountain near Bethlehem. Excavations in 2007 revealed his tomb.

Herod Antipas, the son of Herod the Great, was the ruler of Galilee during Jesus' ministry. Pilate sent Jesus to Herod to be judged, but Herod sent him back to Pilate, who then condemned him. One of his palaces was at Machaerus, in Jordan on the northeast side of the Dead Sea. According to first century historian Josephus, this was the palace where Herod beheaded John the Baptist.

The Herodium

The dungeon at Machaerus

Although the Romans crucified thousands of people, finding the remains of victims is rare. Their bodies weren't always given back to the families to bury. During times of unrest, the bodies were left on the cross to rot. Other times they were thrown into shallow graves or trash heaps. In 1968, construction workers happened to find an ossuary containing the bones of a crucifixion victim. An inscription on the box identified him as "Yohannan," and he was in his mid-20s. A nail was still piercing one of the ankle bones.

Crucifixion Victim
Date: 1st century AD
Location: Jerusalem, Israel
Discovered: 1968
Museum: Israel Museum, Jerusalem

Jesus' World

Capernaum
and
Galilee

Capernaum before excavation

Peter's House
Date: c.2nd cent BC -
1st cent. AD
Location: Capernaum
Discovered: 1968

Fisherman on Galilee

Galilee Boat
Date: c.120 BC – AD 40
Location: Sea of Galilee
Discovered: 1986
Museum: Egyptian Yigal
Allon Museum, Kibbutz
Ginnosar, Israel

Capernaum was the headquarters for the Galilean ministry of Jesus. When the ruins of the town were excavated, the walls of a strange, octagonal building were found surrounding it and built on top of a particular house. The octagonal walls were from a church built in the 5th century. It was an enlargement of a previous church from the 4th century. The house it was built on was from the late Hellenistic period that had become a house church in the late 1st century AD. Many inscriptions were found on the site mentioning Jesus as God, and also mentioning Peter. The best explanation for this particular house being used as a church in the 1st century is that it was Peter's house, where Jesus would stay.

A drought in the mid 1980s revealed a boat submerged in mud on the bank of the Sea of Galilee. The boat is dated between 120 BC and AD 40. It's the same kind of boat Jesus and his disciples would have used to travel across the lake and to fish with.

Pool of Bethesda

Date: c. 1st cent AD
Location: Jerusalem
Discovered: 1888

A couple of the pools where Jesus performed healings have been found in Jerusalem. The pools were lost because they had been filled in and built on top of. But with the restoration of buildings near the pools, or as new construction began, the pools were found.

The pool of Bethesda was found next to the Church of St. Anne. This is the place where Jesus healed a bedridden man in John 5.

The Pool of Siloam (where Jesus healed a blind man in John 9) was partially recovered in the discovery of Hezekiah's tunnel. But the full pool with its trapezoidal shape was not

Pool of Siloam
Date: c.1st cent AD
Location: Jerusalem
Discovered: 2005

The Pool of Siloam [:] Piscine de Siloé.

uncovered until 2005.
Evidence for the Roman
Emperors who ruled during
Jesus' lifetime is seen in many
different archaeological finds.
The most common finds are
probably the coins minted during
their reigns.
When Jesus was born, the
emperor was Caesar Augustus,
who ruled from 27 BC to AD
14.
Apart from the story of
Jesus' birth, whenever the
gospels mention Caesar, they
are referring to Tiberius Caesar.
When Jesus asks whose image
and inscription is on the denarius
in Matthew 22:20, Mark 12:16
and Luke Luke 20:24, the
answer is Tiberius Caesar.

Tiberius Coin
Date: AD 17-34
Museum: Archaeological
Park, La Mancha, Spain

Augustus Coin
Date: 27BC - AD 14
Museum: Cabinet des
médailles, Paris

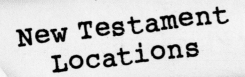

New Testament Locations

Excavation at Corinth in 1898

In addition to the gospels, the New Testament records the teachings of the Apostles as they spread the good news around the Mediterranean world. It can be easy to forget that most of the books of the New Testament aren't books at all, but letters to churches in different cities or to certain people. And the letters mention many other places the Apostles traveled. Revelation itself contains seven separate letters to different places. Although the New Testament is far more than a history book, it does contain history. Like the Old Testament, the New Testament has been an extremely valuable tool for archaeology. In fact, even archaeologists who are not interested in Christianity have appreciated the accuracy of its history.

Mamertine prison in Rome, where tradition says both Peter and Paul were held before their executions.

Gaius and Aristarchus, who travelled with Paul, were dragged in this theater at Ephesus in Acts 19:29.

The Areopagus (Mars Hill) in Athens, where Paul gave his famous speech in Acts 17:16-34.

Paul wrote Philippians to the church in the city of Philippi (which is in modern day Greece). Acts also records his visit there.

In Revelation, John wrote letters to seven churches. All of them are real places that can still be seen. One of them was Pergamum. This photo is of the foundation of the temple there that was moved to the Pergamum Museum in Berlin.

New Testament Inscriptions

Politarch Inscription

Date: c, 2nd century AD
Location: Thessalonika
Discovered: 1876
Museum: British Museum, London

In the past, Luke's writings in particular were attacked by skeptics because the terminology he used (such as the titles of local rulers) wasn't found outside of his work. However, there have been many finds that show Luke's terms were accurate and that he was referring to hisorically verifiable people. As a result, today Luke is held in high regard as a historian.

Between 1877 and 1887, three different inscriptions from the first century were found containing the name Sergius Paulus. Two were found on Cyrpus, the other in Rome. A fourth was found in 1912 in Turkey, but may refer to his son or another man with the same name. These agree with Luke's account in Acts 13 that a man named Sergius Paulus was proconsul on Cyprus around Paphos.

Sergius Paulus Inscription

Date: 1st century AD
Location: Antioch, Turkey
Discovered: 1912
Museum: Yalvac Museum, Turkey

Erastus Inscription

Date: 1st century AD
Location: Corinth, Greece
Discovered: 1929

Gallio Inscription

Date: mid 1st century AD
Location: Delphi, Greece
Discovered: 1905
Museum: Delphi Museum, Greece

In Acts 17:6 Luke calls the rulers at Thessalonika "politarchs." 32 inscriptions mentioning "politarchs" have been found, 19 of them from Thessalonika.

The name "Erastus" was found in a paving stone in Corinth. Luke mentions Erastus in Acts 19. He is also referred to in Romans 16:23 and 2 Timothy 4:20.

The Gallio inscription is important because it says the same thing as Acts 18:12 – that Gallio was proconsul of Achaia. It's also important because it says he was in office from 51-53. This helps date Paul's second missionary journey with more accuracy.

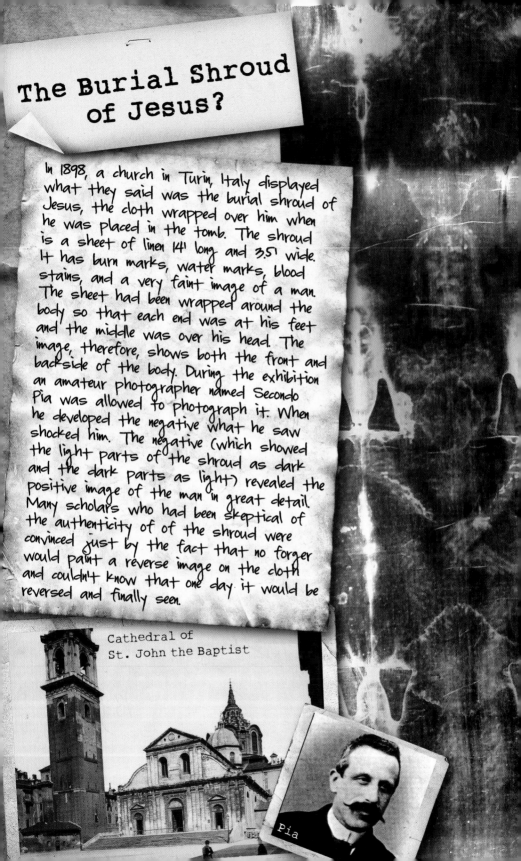

The Burial Shroud of Jesus?

In 1898, a church in Turin, Italy displayed what they said was the burial shroud of Jesus, the cloth wrapped over him when he was placed in the tomb. The shroud is a sheet of linen 14' long and 3.5' wide. It has burn marks, water marks, blood stains, and a very faint image of a man. The sheet had been wrapped around the body so that each end was at his feet and the middle was over his head. The image, therefore, shows both the front and backside of the body. During the exhibition an amateur photographer named Secondo Pia was allowed to photograph it. When he developed the negative what he saw shocked him. The negative (which showed the light parts of the shroud as dark and the dark parts as light) revealed the positive image of the man in great detail. Many scholars who had been skeptical of the authenticity of of the shroud were convinced just by the fact that no forger would paint a reverse image on the cloth and couldn't know that one day it would be reversed and finally seen.

Cathedral of
St. John the Baptist

Pia

The image shows some very interesting things that a forger would probably not include and/or could not know to include. The shoulders of the man have been dislocated, making his arms at least six inches longer than if they had been in place. The nail wounds are through his wrists rather than his hands (as shown in medieval images of the crucifixion). When the nails go through the wrist the damage to the median nerve makes the thumbs turn inward tightly, something a medieval forger would not know. Also, the body is in a state of rigor mortis. Two additional features are especially noteworthy: The image on the shroud actually shows bone structure inside the body much like an X-ray. The bones of the fingers can be seen in the palm. And even though his mouth is shut, his teeth (including the roots) can be seen. The image has a three-dimensional quality that enables scientists to use the information to create a computer model of the man. The second noteworthy thing is that there are coins on the man's eyes. When this was first discovered some people thought this was evidence of forgery because there was a misspelled word on the coin. However, since finding the coins in the image several coins have been discovered that show the same misspelling on the same coin. And that coin, a lepton, was minted in Judea by Pontius Pilate between AD 29 and 32.

As for what is making the image, it is not paint or some other kind of stain or dye. The image is only on the surface of the outer strands of the material and do not penetrate the cloth as pigment would. The image is not on the reverse side of the shroud. It's also not distorted. If the image was made by laying it on a body then the image would become distorted when it was laid flat. The image would only look correct when overlaying the shape of a body. But the image on the shroud is not distorted at all. It's more like a photograph. The blood stains are definitely contact stains, but the image was not made by contact. Imaging tests by scientists from Jet Propulsion Laboratory found that the image has no direction, meaning it has no brushstrokes.

The linen sheet itself contains clues about its origin. Spores from 49 different plants have been found on the material. Of those, 33 of these plants are not found in Europe, but are from Turkey and Palestine. The linen itself is a weave that was often found in the 1st century Mideast. There is also some evidence the same loom that wove the shroud was also used with cotton, which is not grown in Europe..

The Burial Shroud of Jesus?
continued

The shroud's first known appearance was in about 1357. Even then it was controversial, especially because it belonged to a not very distinguished French family. Only after it had been acquired by a more prominent family did it gain acceptability. And eventually it ended up at the church in Turin in 1578. Before that time it was not known as the Shroud of Turin, of course, so history would have referred to it by other names. A good case can be made for it being the same cloth as what is known as the Mandylion. This was a cloth that was discovered hidden in a wall in Edessa (in Turkey) in 525 and said to show the image of Christ. Copies made of it bear a strong resemblance to the face on the shroud. By 1204 it had been moved to Constantinople where it disappeared during the sacking of the city in the Fourth Crusade.

From then until 1357 there is a silent period. However, it may have been in the care of the Knights Templar during that time. Their secret ceremonies included something referred to as the "head," and the promise of a glimpse of God, which they worshipped. A recent discovery of a painting of the head of Christ in the ruins of a Templar building shows a strong similarity to copies of the Mandylion and to the Shroud of Turin. When the Templars were forcibly disbanded, their second in command, a man named Geoffrey de Charnay, was executed in 1314. 43 years later the shroud was displayed by the widow of a man named Geoffrey de Charny. It is not known if these two men were related, but the closeness of their names may be the link that ties the Mandylion and the shroud. The Mandylion is thought of as just the head of Jesus, but a few Byzantine writings hint that the cloth was folded so that only the face was showing and that it was mounted in some kind of frame.

The earliest mention of the shroud outside of the Bible comes from the

Some historians have noted that there is a very standard way of rendering Jesus' face that seems to start around the time the Mandylion was found at Edessa. There are over a dozen unusual features that occur frequently in these images. These include a line or streak across his throat, a line at the base of the neck, a forked beard, and a strange triangular shape at the base of the nose. The reversed image discovered by Pia shows the man in the shroud didn't actually have a forked beard, but it only looks that way because the beard was tucked under a cloth holding the jaw in place. The line at the base of the neck is created by blood held in the bottom of a long beard – something not seen in the other images sharing these other features. Apparently, artists were using the same reference for what Jesus looked like. And this reference seems to have become known in the 6th century.

second century. Prior to 525 there is a story of the king of Edessa, Agbar V, writing to Jesus to come cure him of leprosy. Although Jesus did not come, a disciple came after Jesus died and brought a cloth bearing Jesus' image. Whether or not this story is true, there really was a king Agbar and Edessa did become Christianized for a short time. But Agbar's son did not share his father's faith. When Agbar died and Edessa reverted to paganism, the cloth disappeared. Whether the cloth found hidden at Edessa is the same one as in the story cannot be proven. Whether it is the same cloth that may have been used in worship by the Templars is not known. And whether de Charnay and de Charny are related is not known. But there is enough of a connection to say the shroud may have been known before it was displayed in 1357.

DATING THE SHROUD

An attempt to **definitively** date the shroud was done through radiocarbon testing by labs at the University of Arizona, Oxford, and Institut für Mittelenergiephysik in Zurich. The result showed a 95% degree of confidence that the shroud dated between 1260 and 1390. This seemed to **prove** it was a medieval fake. However, further testing done at Los Alamos in 2004 showed the sample material was taken from a patch on the shroud, not from the original material. The shroud has several places that have been repaired by patches. Additional testing has not been done since.

BIBLIOGRAPHY

Archaeology and the Bible, Volume II, Shanks, Hershel and Dan P. Cole, eds. (Washington D.C.: Biblical Archaeology Society, 1990)

Archaeologial Study Bible (Grand Rapids: Zondervan, 2005)

Ashton, John and David Down. *Unwrapping the Pharaohs* (Green Forest, AR: Masterbooks, 2006)

Bowman, Robert. *Scripture: Authority, Canon, and Criticism*, Syllabus for CSAP529 (La Mirada, CA: Biola University Bookstore)

Boyd, Robert D. *Tells, Tombs and Treasures* (New York: Bonanza, 1969)

Caldwell, Penny Cox. *God of the Mountain* (Alachua, FL: Bridge-Logos, 2008)

Complete Works of Josephus, William Whitson, ed. (Grand Rapids: Kregel, 1960)

Cornuke, Robert. *In Search of the Mountain of God: The Discovery of the Real Mt. Sinai* (Nashville: Broadman & Holman Publishers, 2000)

Dictionary of Biblical Archaeology, Blaiklock, E.M. and R.K. Harrison eds. (Grand Rapids: Zondervan, 1983)

David, Rosalie. *The Pyramid Builders of Ancient Egypt* (London: Routlege & Kegan Paul, 1986)

Fant, Clyde E. and Mitchell G. Reddish. *Lost Treasures of the Bible* (Grand Rapids: Eerdmans, 2008).

Franz, Gordon. "Is Mount Sinai in Saudi Arabia?" *Bible and Spade*, Fall 2000.

Franz, Gordon. "Mount Sinai is NOT Jebel al-Lawz in Saudi Arabia." A paper presented at the annual meeting of the Evangelical Theological Society/Near Eastern Archaeology Society, 15 November 2001.

Free, Joseph P. and Howard F. Vos. *Archaeology and Bible History* (Grand Rapids: Zondervan, 1950, 1992).

Geisler, Norman, and Thomas Howe. *When Critics Ask* (Grand Rapids: Baker, 1992)

Geisler, Norman, and Frank Turek. *I Don't Have Enough Faith to be an Atheist* (Wheaton: Crossway, 2004)

Habermas, Gary. "The Shroud of Turin and its Significance for Biblical Studies" in *Journal of the Evangelical Theological Society* 24:1 (1981): 47-54.

Habermas, Gary and Kenneth E. Stevenson. *Verdict on the Shroud* (Ann Arbor, MI: Servant: 1981)

Harrison, R.K. *Archaeology of the New Testament* (New York: Association Press, 1964)

Heller, John. *Report on the Shroud of Turin* (Boston: Houghton Mifflin, 1983)

Holden, Joseph. *Archaeology and the Bible* PowerPoint Presentation (2010)

Kitchen, Kenneth. *On the Reliability of the Old Testament* (Grand Rapids: Eerdmans, 2003)

Mazarin, Amihai. *Archaeology of the Land of the Bible* (New York: Doubleday, 1990, 1992)

Moller, Lennart. *The Exodus Case* (Copenhagen: Scandinavia Publishing House, 2000, 2008)

Price, Randall. *Secrets of the Dead Sea Scrolls* (Eugene, OR: Harvest House, 1996)

Ritmeyer, Leen and Kathleen Ritmeyer. *Secrets of Jerusalem's Temple Mount* (Washington D.C.: Biblical Archaeology Society, 1998)

Rogers, Raymond N. "Studies on the Radiocarbon Sample from the Shroud of Turin" in *Thermochimica Acta*, Volume 425, Issues 1-2, 20 January 2005, Pages 189-194

Roll, David. *A Test of Time* (London: Arrow, 1995)

Roll, David. *Legend: The Genesis of Civilization* (London: Arrow, 1998, 1999)

Shanks, Hershel. *Understanding the Dead Sea Scrolls* (New York: Random House, 1992)

Unger, Merrill F. *Archaeology and the Old Testament* (Grand Rapids: Zondervan, 1975)

Velikovsky, Immanuel. *Ages in Chaos* (London: London, 1952, 1973)

Vos, Howard. *Archaeology in Bible Lands* (Chicago: Moody Press, 1977)

Vos, Howard. *An Introduction to Biblical Archaeology* (Chicago: Moody, 1956, 1983)

Whittaker, Charles A. "The Biblical Significance of Jabal Al Lawz." Ph.D. dissertation, Louisiana Baptist University, 2003.

Wood, Bryant. "Dating Jericho's Destruction: Bienkowski is Wrong on All Counts" <http://www.biblearchaeology.org/post/2012/03/28/Dating-Jerichos-Destruction-Bienkowski-is-Wrong-on-All-Counts.aspx> (Accessed 12.08.12)

Wood, Bryant. "Did the Israelites Conquer Jericho? A New Look at the Archaeological Evidence."
Biblical Archaeological Review, Vol. XVI, No. 2, March/April 1990, pp44-58. <http://www.biblearchaeology.org/post/2008/05/Did-the-Israelites-Conquer-Jericho-A-New-Look-at-the-Archaeological-Evidence.aspx#Article> (Accessed 12.08.12)

Wood, Bryant. "Thoughts on Jebel al-Lawz as the Location of Mount Sinai." *Bible and Spade*, 17 May 20 <http://www.biblearchaeology.org/post/2006/05/17/Thoughts-on-Jebel-al-Lawz-as-the-Location-of-Mount-Sinai.aspx> (Accessed 12.1.12)

Yamauchi, Edwin. *The Stones and the Scriptures* (Philadelphia: Holman, 1972)

Zondervan Pictorial Encyclopedia of the Bible (Grand Rapids: Zonderzan, 1975, 1976)

IMAGES

COVER) Bible and map: (Public Domain); Elastic band and stamps:
© Photoxpress; Notebook: © iStockphoto; Book spine and Photos: (Public
Domain); Postcard and tape: ©Photoxpress; Tag: © ba1969

INTERIOR BACKGROUND) Paper: iStockphoto.com; Subject labels:
© ba1969

TITLE PAGE) Compass, dirt, and taped paper: ©Photoxpress; Maps and
photos: (Public Domain); Photo frame and small taped paper: ©
iStockphoto; Stapled paper: © ba1969; Torn paper: © SXC;

FLOOD) Atrahasis: Jack1956 (Public Domain); Atrahasis paper: © Baltar
Flood map: C.V. Monin (Public Domain); Gilgamesh Epic: © Mike Peel
(www.mikepeel.com); Gilgamesh statue photo: waitscm (CC-BY-SA 2.0);
King List Pages: Public Domain; Noah's Ark Etching: Gustave Doré
(Public Domain); Rassam Portrait: Public Domain; Tags, open notebook,
and Gilgamesh cover and pages: © ba1969; Water: Mr. Sean Linehan,
NOAA, NGS, Remote Sensing (Public Domain); Weld-Blundell Prism: ©
Ashmolean Museum, University of Oxford

NOAH'S ARK) Ararat: Mediacrat (CC-BY-SA-3.0); Ararat anomaly: Public
Domain; Cudi Dagh: Gertrude Bell, courtesy of The Gertrude Bell
Archive, Newcastle University (catalog number M70); Drogue Stone:
Robert C. Michelson (CC-BY-SA-3.0); Durupinar:
© P.Fabian/Shutterstock; Map: Heinrich_Kiepert (Public Domain);
Mountains of Ararat: © burakalsan/iStockphoto.com; Notebooks and
yarn: © Photoxpress.com; Pins: ©iStockphoto; Satellite photo: Jacques
Descloitres, MODIS Rapid Response Team, NASA-GSFC (Public Domain);
Satellite photo frame (Public Domain)

EGYPT & EXODUS) Amarna paper: ©1042562; Amarna tablet: Rama (CC-BY-SA
2.0); Amenemhet III: sailko (CC-BY-SA 3.0); Brush: Hans Bernhard
(CC-BY-SA-3.0); Ipuwer Papyrus: © Dutch National Museum of
Antiquities (CC-BY-3.0); Jericho: Tamar Hayardeni (CC-BY-SA 3.0);
Kahun map: Flinders Petrie (Public Domain); Kahun paper, Mummy of
Rameses II, Standard chronology paper, Revised chronology paper
and cover: Library of Congress (Public Domain); Maps of Egypt and
Exodus (Public Domain); Pharaoh notebook: © Omernos; Photo frame:
©belterz/iStockphoto; Pyramid of Sesostris II: Einsamer Schütze
(CC-BY-SA-3.0)

MT. SINAI?) Bovine petroglyphs, pillars, and warning sign: © Aaron Sen;
Bovine petroglyph, Cave, Golden Calf altar, Jebel al Maqla, Pillar,
"V" altar: © Jim and Penny Caldwell; Notebooks: © Photoxpress; Paper:
© ba1969; Satellite photo: Jacques Descloitres, MODIS Rapid Response
Team, NASA-GSFC (Public Domain); Spiral notebook: © rawku5

DAVID, YHWH, ISRAEL INSCRIPTIONS) Amarah-West and Soleb: Francis Frith
(Public Domain); Diary: Library of Congress (Public Domain); Diary
page, map back, paper scraps, and tags © ba1969; Maps: Palistine and
Egypt by Heinrich Kiepert (Public Domain); Nile by Lepsius (Public
Domain); Nineveh pages: © MsDotty; Merneptah Stele: © Todd Bolen;
Mesha Stele by Paterm (CC-BY-SA 3.0); Portraits of Clermont-Ganneau,
Petrie, and Warren (Public Domain); Tel Dan by Ani Nimi (Public
Domain); Tel Dan Inscription © House of Peace

SENNACHERIB'S SEIGE) Aerial photo of Jerusalem, Beginning of tunnel, and
Lachish: Matson Photograph collection (Public Domain); Hezekiah's
tunnel inscription and Pool of Siloam: American Colony Photo Dept.
(Public Domain); Jerusalem book: © liuhuan; Jerusalem book pages:
© magicmarie; Nineveh book and Tags © ba1969: Photo frames: ©
iStockphoto; Map: Spruner (Public Domain); Sennacharib's Palace at
British Museum: Mujtaba Chohan (CC-BY-SA 3.0); Sennacherib's Prism:
David Castor (Public Domain); Tool: Hannibal21 (CC-BY-SA 3.0)

THANKS

John Bloom, Ted Wright, Jim and Penny Caldwell, Bill Crouse, Jeremy Howard, Randall Price, Aaron Sen, Steve Bond, GB Howell, Jr., Frank Turek, Gary Habermas, David Filson, Richard and Gwen Powell, Jules and Mia Powell, Davis Carman, Zan Tyler.

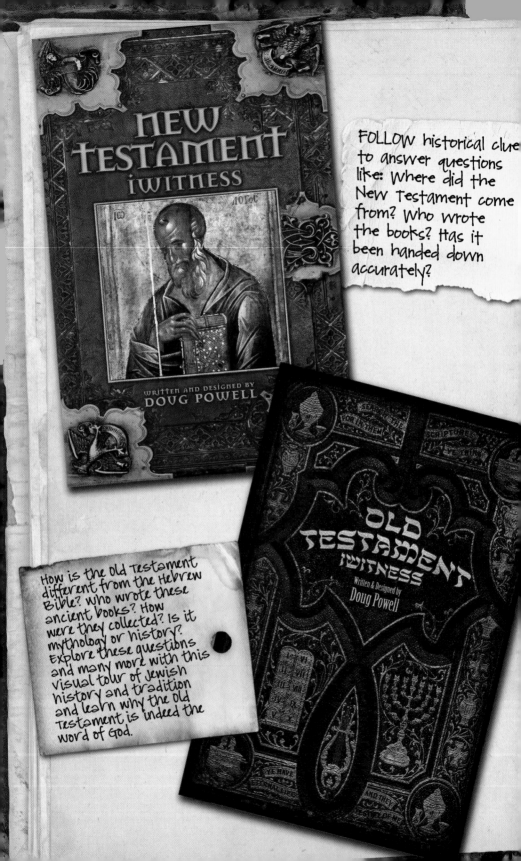

NEW TESTAMENT iWITNESS

WRITTEN AND DESIGNED BY
DOUG POWELL

FOLLOW historical clue to answer questions like: Where did the New Testament come from? Who wrote the books? Has it been handed down accurately?

How is the Old Testament different from the Hebrew Bible? Who wrote these ancient books? How were they collected? Is it mythology or history? Explore these questions and many more with this visual tour of Jewish history and tradition and learn why the Old Testament is indeed the word of God.

OLD TESTAMENT iWITNESS

Written & Designed by
Doug Powell